At the Mall

by Kimberly Irving
illustrated by Meryl Henderson

Core Decodable 20

Bothell, WA • Chicago, IL • Columbus, OH • New York, NY

MHEonline.com

Copyright © 2015 McGraw-Hill Education

All rights reserved. No part of this publication may be reproduced or distributed in any form or by any means, or stored in a database or retrieval system, without the prior written consent of McGraw-Hill Education, including, but not limited to, network storage or transmission, or broadcast for distance learning.

Send all inquiries to:
McGraw-Hill Education
8787 Orion Place
Columbus, OH 43240

ISBN: 978-0-02-132626-6
MHID: 0-02-132626-6

Printed in the United States of America.

2 3 4 5 6 7 8 9 DOC 20 19 18 17 16 15

Dad sits in a mall.

Dad has a list.

4

Is it a small ball?

Dad is calm.

"I can call Mom," Dad said.

Dad did call.
Mom is at the mall!

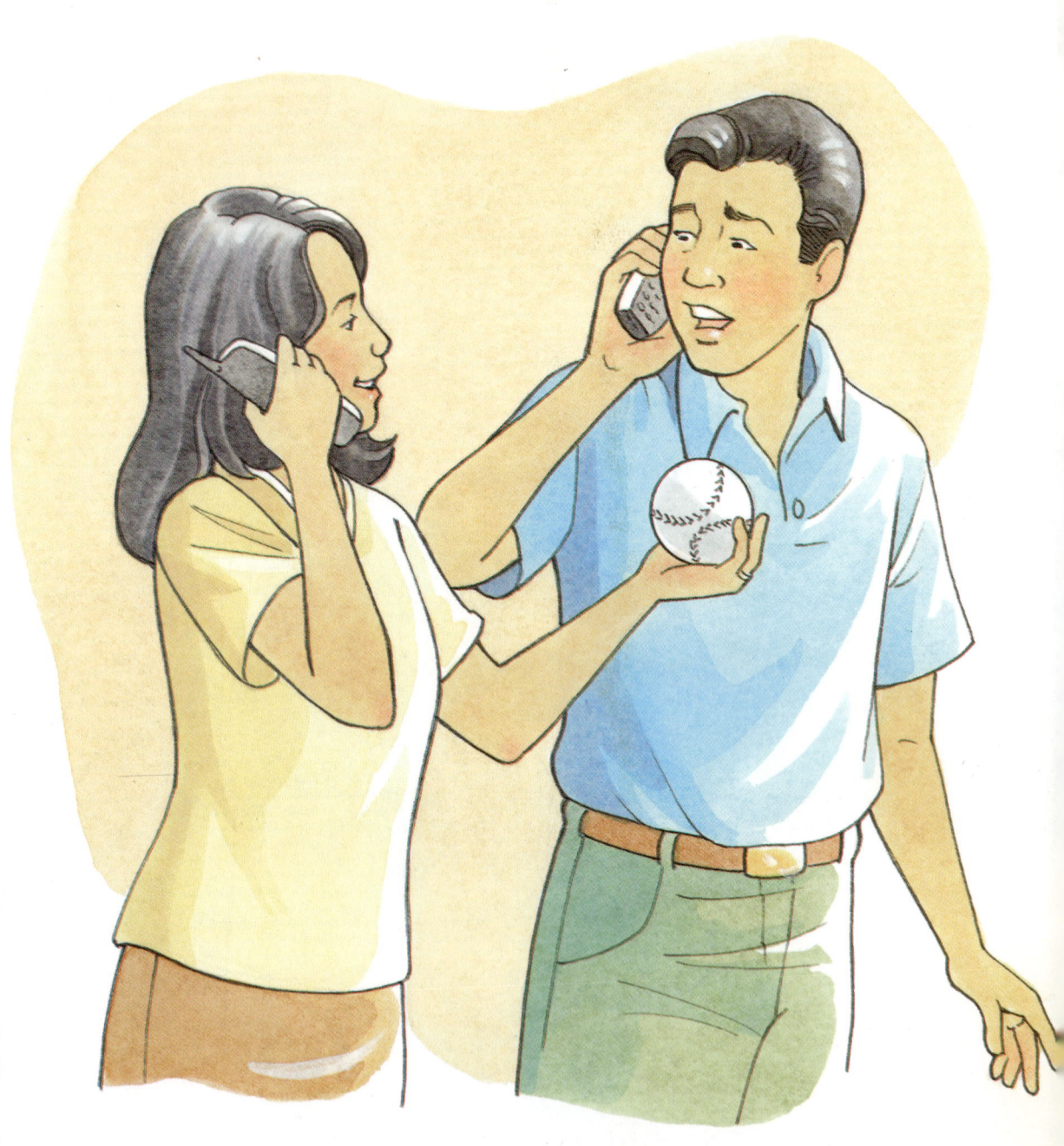

"It is a small ball," said Mom.